LITTLE CHIMPANZEE

words&pictures

© 2023 Quarto Publishing Group USA Inc.
Text © 2023 Anna Brett
Illustrations © 2023 Rebeca Pintos

First published in 2023 by words & pictures,
an imprint of The Quarto Group.
100 Cummings Center,
Suite 265D Beverly, MA 01915, USA.
T (978) 282-9590 F (978) 283-2742
www.quarto.com

Assistant Editor: Alice Hobbs
Art Director: Susi Martin
Designer: Clare Barber
Publisher: Holly Willsher

A CIP record for this book is available from the Library of Congress.

ISBN: 978-0-7112-8358-9

9 8 7 6 5 4 3 2 1

Manufactured in Guangdong, China TT032023

LITTLE CHIMPANZEE

ANNA BRETT

illustrated by
REBECA PINTOS

Good morning!
I'm Little Chimpanzee and
I'd love it if you stayed and
played with me today.

I'll introduce you to my family and we can explore my African rain forest home together. As the sun is rising, let's climb up into the trees and wake everyone up.

Rise and shine everyone! This is my family, and as a group we are called a community. My dad is the alpha male and head of the family.

My mom looks after me and my older brother, while my aunts, uncles, and cousins make up the rest of the community.

Like the rest of my family, I have long black hair covering most of my body, but my face, ears, hands, and feet are hairless and will get darker as I age.

I always stay close
to my mom and I
love to ride on her
back as we explore
the rain forest.

When I was tiny
I clung on to the
fur on her tummy.

My brother is nearly five years
old and is getting more independent now,
but he's still not old enough to leave our
community—or our mom—yet!

We spend most of our time up
in the trees and get around by
swinging from branch to branch.

Our arms are very strong and very long—
they reach down to our knees. It's fun to
practice hanging one-handed, and I'm
brave enough now to let go in mid-air
when *swinging between branches!*

I'm hungry—time to look for a morning snack. We mostly eat fruit, nuts, and seeds.

Mom is teaching me how to forage among the leaves for tasty bites.

Occasionally we'll hunt for insects too. Ants are fun to fish out of their nests with a stick. If we get too sticky with fruit juice or ants, we grab a leaf and wipe ourselves clean.

When I need a drink I collect leaves
or a clump of moss and soak up water
from the ground like a sponge. Slurp!

We also like to splash in
the river to cool down when
the temperature rises.

It's the middle of the day and the sun is at its hottest so it's time for us to have a rest.

Mom brushes my fur and picks out any dirt in a process called grooming.

She uses her lips
as well as her fingers
to remove specks.

My aunt grooms her
while she grooms me!

It's very relaxing and we
often stay like this for hours.

Even when we are resting we still need to keep a lookout for predators like leopards and snakes.

Mom has warned us
that leopards may grab
baby chimps if we stray
away from the group, and
many rain forest snakes
are venomous.

The adults shout out
an alarm to alert the
community if they spot
anything dangerous.

My dad is the alpha male of our community, which means he's the leader.

His duties involve protecting us by patrolling the boundaries of our home range and maintaining his status as number one by fighting off rival aggressive males.

We always rush to welcome him
back when he's been away.

This afternoon Mom is showing me how to use stones as hammers to crack nuts out of their shells.

We use a hard, flat base to place the nut on, and then we try different shaped stones to see which works best.

I'm also learning how to carefully use my hands and fingers to remove the shell once it's cracked.

Tasty kola and palm nuts are the
reward for our hard work!

We use our hands and bodies
as well as facial expressions and
noises to talk to each other. By
combining these, we can communicate
any message we need to.

24

We also know that sharing is caring, and any food we discover is shared equally.

I love to give my family big hugs and kisses to show them that I love them.

When it's time for a mom to have a baby, they disappear from the group and find a safe space to hide and give birth in. They do this on their own, often under the cover of darkness, for safety and privacy.

My aunt is returning with her new baby today. She's been on "maternity leave" from the group for a month.

Before the end of the day approaches, it's time to move to a new spot to find some more food. After traveling through the trees for a while, we head down to the ground.

Since our arms are so long, we're a bit unsteady when standing fully upright! So instead, we walk on all fours and use our knuckles to support our weight and keep us stable.

29

Now that we've reached a new area of the rain forest, it's time to build our nests for tonight. We collect branches and weave them together with leaves to make a comfy base high up in the trees.

I like to add in a couple of flowers as well! We'll use these nests for a few nights until we move to a new area once again.

Yawn! The sun has set and it's now time for sleep. We love to recharge for up to nine hours each night.

I hope you've enjoyed spending the day
with me and my family and have seen
that life as a chimpanzee is so much fun!
Goodnight, friends.

FUN FACTS

Thank you for swinging
through the trees with
me today—it was great fun.
While I sit down for some
grooming with Mom, let me tell
you some more facts
about chimpanzees.

Young chimpanzee

- Chimpanzees are not picky eaters—they love fruit but eat insects and meat too.

- They are part of a group called the "great apes." It also includes gorillas, bonobos, orangutans—and humans!

- Females give birth every 5–6 years and typically have three children across their lifetime.

- Chimpanzees don't have a tail.

- Wild chimpanzees can only be found in Africa.

- Chimpanzees like to keep their nests very clean, which is why they rebuild them almost every night.

Young chimpanzee swinging from a tree

Chimpanzee relaxing in their nest

FACT FILE

Weight: 55–154 pounds

Height: 4–5.5 feet

Lifespan: Around 30–50 years in the wild

MOM AND BABY BONDING

Little Chimpanzee's mom is preparing a tasty snack—she fishes termites out of a mound using a twig. Can you count how many she has caught? And how many is Little Chimpanzee about to gobble up?

Baby chimps stay close to their moms for the first few years of their life. These youngsters have been playing, but it's now time for them to hitch a piggyback ride home. Can you match each baby to its mom?

CHIMP CONSERVATION

Sadly, chimpanzees are classified as an endangered species. This means their numbers are dropping and we must protect them to prevent future extinction, which would mean there were no more left in the wild.

In 1900 there were an estimated one million chimpanzees, but today there are as few as 340,000. This is mainly because their rain forest habitats are being destroyed due to agriculture and logging. Hunting is also an issue, as well as disease.

But there are ways we can help. We can support charities that help with conservation. This is where habitats are protected to provide endangered animals with a safe place to live. Local communities are also helped and educated about how to

The rest of my species and I are sadly endangered. But there are ways people can help us!

live peacefully alongside animals, while still making a living from the rain forest's resources.

Sanctuaries and wildlife centers are other important ways humans can help endangered

Sign at the entrance to a sanctuary in Sierra Leone

Young chimpanzee with carer at a sanctuary

chimpanzees. The Pan African Sanctuary Alliance has 23 sanctuaries and wildlife centers in 13 countries across Africa. They are able to rescue and rehabilitate chimpanzees, particularly orphans and those that need medical attention.

CHIMPS UP CLOSE!

This group are grooming each other. Some of the little ones have lots of bugs in their fur after a morning in the treetops! Can you spot five differences between these before and after pictures?

One of the chimpanzees in this community is not quite like the others. Can you spot the odd one out?

HAND PRINT CHIMP

Chimpanzees love to swing! Create some cute handprint chimps doing acrobatics in the trees following the simple steps below.

YOU WILL NEED

- Large piece of paper
- Brown and black paint
- Two paintbrushes
- Black marker
- Green marker

1 Paint the four fingers and the palm of one hand in black paint. Be sure to keep your thumb clean!

2 Press your painted hand down on the left side of your paper. This has created your chimpanzee's body and limbs.

3 Close the same hand into a fist and paint the outside area of the top of your fist black. This is the fur on the head. Then paint the inside area brown, to make the chimp's face.

4 Print your fist where you left the thumb space on your handprint. Then using the paintbrushes, paint on two ears—black on the outside and brown in the center.

5 Once the paint has dried, use the black pen to draw your chimpanzee's face—two eyes, two little nostrils, and a big smile.

6 Next, using the green pen, draw a branch for the chimp's arms to hang on to.

7 Repeat the steps to add more chimpanzees to your picture. Try printing your hand at different angles to create chimps swinging in all directions.

NOW YOU CAN MAKE A WHOLE COMMUNITY!

JANE GOODALL AND THE GOMBE CHIMPS

Here's a story about rescue and rehabilitation that helped several of my cousins survive.

Jane Goodall with chimpanzee in Gombe Stream National Park

The reason we know so much about chimpanzees today is largely due to one woman—Dr. Jane Goodall. She began studying the wild chimpanzees in the Gombe Stream National Park in Tanzania more than 60 years ago.

Jane took the time to watch the social and family interactions of a community and realised that like humans, chimpanzees all have individual personalities. She saw how they felt happiness, sadness, and other emotions, just like humans do. She also discovered that chimpanzees ate meat as well as plants.

But her most ground-breaking observation was that chimpanzees know how to make and use tools. It was previously thought that only humans used tools, but she watched in amazement as a chimpanzee used a twig to "fish" for termites in a termite mound. David Greybeard was one of the chimpanzees Jane observed doing this. He became a firm favorite of hers and the two developed a friendship over the years.

Jane Goodall with a young chimpanzee

Jane's legacy means there are now programs around the world focused on inspiring young people to care for wildlife and the planet. And the Jane Goodall Institute means her work will continue for generations to come.

QUIZ

Follow in Jane Goodall's footsteps and become an expert on chimpanzees! If you can score ten out of ten on this quiz, then you're well on your way to knowing all about these amazing animals.

1. Chimpanzees can be found living in the wild all around the world. True or False?

2. Is a male or a female adult chimpanzee the leader of a community?

3. In their first year of life, baby chimps cling to their mom's...
   a) Back
   b) Tummy
   c) Back and tummy

4. What do chimpanzees use to help them crack open nuts?

The answers are on page 48.

5. Chimpanzees walk on two legs when on the ground. True or false?

6. Do chimpanzees sleep at night or in the day?

7. How do chimpanzees alert others to danger from predators?
   a) Hide
   b) Shout out an alarm call
   c) Wave tree branches like a flag

8. The process by which different chimps clean each other's fur is called...?

9. Do chimpanzees swing using their arms or their legs?

10. Chimps have a tail. True or false?

ANSWERS

P36 Mum has caught 15 termites and Little Chimpanzee has 5.

P37 a=1, b=5, c=2, d=4, e=3

P40-41

Picture credits
P34 top: Marcel Schauer/ Dreamstime. P35 top: Mattiaath/ Dreamstime, bottom: Minden Pictures / Alamy Stock Photo. P39 top: imageBROKER / Alamy Stock Photo, bottom: Martin Harvey / Getty Images. P44 bottom: Bettmann / Getty Images. P45 top: Avalon/ Bruce Coleman Inc / Alamy Stock Photo. P46 top: Patrick Rolands / Dreamstime. P47 top: Patrick Rolands / Dreamstime, bottom: Antony Souter / Alamy Stock Photo.

1. False—they can only be found in Africa.

2. A male chimpanzee leads the community.

3. Answer c): baby chimps cling to their mom's tummy and back fur in the first year of their life.

4. Rocks and stones.

5. False—they walk on all four limbs.

6. They sleep at night.

7. Answer b): they shout out an alarm call.

8. Grooming.

9. They swing using their arms.

10. False—chimpanzees don't have a tail.